ROOM

A THEATRE ROYAL STRATFORD EAST AND ABBEY THEATRE, DUBLIN
CO-PRODUCTION, IN ASSOCIATION WITH NATIONAL THEATRE OF SCOTLAND
AND COVENT GARDEN PRODUCTIONS

ROOM

BY EMMA DONOGHUE

ADAPTED FOR THE STAGE BY EMMA DONOGHUE

MUSIC AND LYRICS BY CORA BISSETT AND KATHRYN JOSEPH

OBERON BOOKS
LONDON

WWW.OBERONBOOKS.COM

This adaptation first published in 2017 by Oberon Books Ltd
521 Caledonian Road, London N7 9RH
Tel: +44 (0) 20 7607 3637 / Fax: +44 (0) 20 7607 3629
e-mail: info@oberonbooks.com
www.oberonbooks.com

A catalogue record for this book is available from the British
Library.

PB ISBN: 9781786821768
E ISBN: 9781786821775

Cover design by Rebecca Pitt, photography by Scott Rylander

Printed and bound by Marston Book Services, Didcot.
eBook conversion by CPI Group (UK) Ltd, Croydon, CR0 4YY.

Room premiered at Theatre Royal Stratford East on 2 May 2017 before performing at Dundee Rep Theatre (13 – 17 June 2017) and the Abbey Theatre Dublin (24 June – 22 July 2017) with the following cast (in alphabetical order):

GRANDAD/DOCTOR	Stephen Casey
POLICE/INTERVIEWER	Janet Kumah
BIG JACK	Fela Lufadeju
OLD NICK	Liam McKenna
GRAN	Lucy Tregear
MA	Witney White
LITTLE JACK	Darmani Ebojim
	Taye Kassim Junaid-Evans
	Harrison Wilding

Creative Team
Written by: Emma Donoghue
Adapted for the stage by: Emma Donoghue
Music and Lyrics by: Cora Bissett and Kathryn Joseph
Director: Cora Bissett
Designer: Lily Arnold
Video Designer: Andrzej Goulding
Lighting Designer: David Plater
Musical Director: Gavin Whitworth
Sound Designer: Alexandra Faye Braithwaite
Puppet Designer: David Cauchi
Movement Director: Siân Williams
Associate Director: Ellen Havard
Casting Director: Debbie O'Brien

An early workshop of *Room* was developed with Chicago Shakespeare Theater and Richard Jordan Productions.

THEATRE ROYAL
STRATFORD
EAST ...*a people's theatre*

This famous producing theatre, located in the heart of London's East End prides itself on creating world class work that reflects the concerns, hopes and dreams of its community. A prolific developer of new work, this award-winning theatre attracts artists and audiences often not represented in other venues and is firmly committed to supporting the development of exciting new voices and bold new work.

As part of this, the venue's bi-annual Angelic Tales New Writing Festival features rehearsed readings by more than twenty emerging writers and has led to work being developed into full main stage productions and for the last ten years has developed hundreds of new writers of contemporary musical theatre.

Recent staged new productions include Atiha Sen Gupta's *Counting Stars*, Kirsten Childs' *The Bubbly Black Girl Sheds Her Chameleon Skin*, Bonnie Greer's *The Hotel Cerise* and the Ramps On The Moon production of The Who's *Tommy* directed by our Artistic Director Kerry Michael.

Contact us
Theatre Royal Stratford East
Gerry Raffles Square
London E15 1BN

Box office & information
020 8534 0310 Mon-Sat, 10am-6pm
www.stratfordeast.com
theatreroyal@stratfordeast.com

Twitter @stratfordeast
Facebook /theatreroyalstratfordeast

Typetalk 07972 918 050
Administration 020 8534 7374

Supported using public funding by
ARTS COUNCIL ENGLAND

in partnership with

Newham London

**ABBEY
THEATRE
AMHARCLANN
NA MAINISTREACH**

We are Ireland's National Theatre. We belong to the people of Ireland. We tell their story through ambitious, courageous and new theatre in all it's forms.

We stage over thirty plays at our home in Dublin City Centre each year. We tour in Ireland and internationally to bring the best of Irish theatre to as many people as we can.

In our programme you will find new Irish writing, modern classics, adaptations, new versions of classic Irish plays, verbatim theatre, dance and the best of Irish and international theatre, presented in partnership with a growing community of theatre-makers and companies.

Our theatre was founded by revolutionaries, W.B. Yeats and Lady Gregory. They invented a new theatrical tradition in Ireland. We are inspired by their legacy to explore new narratives and horizons for Irish theatre.

We are dedicated to celebrating the vibrant and diverse voices and experiences that exist all over Ireland. Our New Work department invites ideas and scripts from theatre-makers at all career stages.

With tickets starting at 13 euro and early bird tickets and free previews, our Arts Council funding helps us maintain affordable ticket prices.

The Abbey is a place for artists and audiences to come together. Join us at your national theatre.

An Roinn Ealaíon, Oidhreachta,
Gnóthaí Réigiúnacha, Tuaithe agus Gaeltachta

Department of Arts, Heritage,
Regional, Rural and Gaeltacht Affairs

The Abbey Theatre is funded by the Arts Council / An Chomhairle Ealaíon and receives financial assistance from the Department of Arts, Heritage, Regional, Rural and Gaeltacht Affairs

NATIONAL THEATRE OF SCOTLAND

The National Theatre of Scotland was established in 2006 and has created over 200 productions. Being a theatre without walls, the Company presents a wide variety of work that ranges from large-scale productions to projects tailored to the smallest performing spaces. In addition to conventional theatres, the Company has performed in airports, schools, tower blocks, community halls, ferries and forests.

The Company has toured extensively across Scotland, the rest of the UK and worldwide. Notable productions include *Black Watch* by Gregory Burke which won four Olivier Awards amongst a multitude of awards, the award-winning landmark historical trilogy *The James Plays* by Rona Munro, a radical reimagining of *Macbeth* starring Alan Cumming, presented in Glasgow and at the Lincoln Center Festival and subsequently, Broadway, New York and the Olivier Award winning *Our Ladies of Perpetual Succour*, playing in London's West End from May to September 2017.

The National Theatre of Scotland creates much of its work in partnership with theatre-makers, companies, venues and participants across the globe. From extraordinary projects with schools and communities, to the groundbreaking online 5 Minute Theatre to immersive pieces such as David Greig's *The Strange Undoing of Prudencia Hart*, the National Theatre of Scotland's aspiration is to tell the stories that need to be told and to take work to wherever audiences are to be found.

Artistic Director and Chief Executive: **Jackie Wylie**

Chair: **Seona Reid DBE**

For the latest information on all our activities, visit us online at
nationaltheatrescotland.com

Covent Garden

PRODUCTIONS

Covent Garden Productions is a theatrical production and live entertainment company, set up to create, manage and develop exceptional new work both in the West End and on National Tour.

Productions Include:

BEACHES – a new musical

Book by Iris Rainer Dart & Thom Thomas Music by David Austin Lyrics by Iris Rainer Dart

Directed by Eric Schaeffer

Beaches is a New York Times Best-Selling novel by Iris Rainer Dart. In 1988 it was adapted into the classic, film starring Bette Midler and Barbara Hershey.

NO VILLAIN – world premiere of Arthur Miller's first play

Direction by Sean Turner

No Villain tells the story of a garment industry strike that sets a son against his factory proprietor father. Here, Miller explores the Marxist theory that would see him hauled before the House Un-American Activities Committee years later.

This remarkable debut play gives us a tantalising glimpse of Miller's early life, the seeding of his political values and the beginning of his extraordinary career.

JACKIE THE MUSICAL – UK Tour 2016

Directed by Anna Linstrum

Choreography by Arlene Phillips

Editor in Cheif: Nina Myskow

A whirlwind tour of the 70's celebrating the much loved Jackie Magazine on stages across the UK.

COVENT GARDEN PRODUCTIONS

Producer | Sam Julyan

Producer | Douglas McJannet

Associate Producer | Paul Casey

www.coventgardenproductions.com

Characters

BIG JACK

LITTLE JACK

MA

OLD NICK

GRAN

GRANDAD

POLICE

DOCTOR

INTERVIEWER

ACT ONE

ORDINARY DAY

BIG JACK: When I look up through Skylight there's Outer Space with all the Stars and Planets and Moon and Sun spinning spinning spinning around us. And then way farther up there's Heaven, where I came from when I was the tiniest little speck.

Ma's asleep but I'm awake. The morning after tomorrow morning, I'm going to be five! I'm already big inside. Sometimes I think things that Ma doesn't even hear.

LITTLE JACK: Morning, Ma.

MA: Morning, Jack.

LITTLE JACK: Rise and shine. Morning Room, morning Walls, morning Wardrobe, morning Skylight, morning Plant. Why don't you have flowers anymore?

MA: Maybe she's tired.

LITTLE JACK: *(To plant.)* You should have a nap. Morning Sockdog, morning Labyrinth, morning Lamp, morning Wonky Chair, morning Eggsnake, morning Keypad…ten nine eight seven six five four three two one…blast off!

MA: How many o's will we have for breakfast?

LITTLE JACK: Fifty, each of us, that's a hundred.

MA: What spoon would you like?

LITTLE JACK: Meltedy Spoon.

She hums 'Pop Goes the Weasel'.

BIG JACK: Me and Ma play the humming game. I always know hers.

LITTLE JACK: 'Pop Goes the Weasel!'

BIG JACK: Ma doesn't always guess mine, sometimes she's a dumbo Ma.

MA: Time for vitamins.

BIG JACK: Vitamins are for keeping us well and not dying and going back to Heaven early.

MA spills the last three into her hand.

Just three left.

Worried, MA doles them out.

MA: One for you, one for me. Time for P.E. now. What do you choose?

LITTLE JACK: I choose… Track.

MA: I bet you can do a lap of Room in ten steps.

LITTLE JACK: Nine steps.

MA: Eight.

LITTLE JACK: None!

MA: Ready…

BIG JACK / LITTLE JACK: Steady…

MA: Go! And the young champion's giving it all he's got, today. He's coming up on the outside, he's edging past the pack… Is it possible we're going to see a new world record? Yes, he's smashed it! He's going faster than the speed of sound, faster than the speed of light. Is it a bird, is it a plane? No, it's SuperJack!

Now my turn. I choose… Flying Rug.

They kneel up on Rug.

BIG JACK: We're zooming over a desert.

MA: I see palm trees and camels. Wildebeest and lions and pink flamingos and…

LITTLE JACK: Snails!

MA: There's a mountain and a hot air balloon.

LITTLE JACK: Bicycles and bulldozers.

MA: Here comes the hugest waterfall –

> *They steer over it and plunge down.*

and the sea, and whales spouting…

BIG JACK: And mermaids. Watch out, a skyscraper.

LITTLE JACK / BIG JACK / MA: Argh!

> *They crash into it and fall.*

MA: Okeydokey, Jack?

LITTLE JACK: Hunky-dory, Ma.

MA: It's Monday. You know what that means?

LITTLE JACK: Laundry.

> *They wash their clothes, sheets and towels in Bath, pounding out the dirt.*

BIG JACK: Me and Ma have thousands of jobs to do every day. Rhyming and Dancing and Chopping Up vegetables with Zigzag Knife. Darning holes in our clothes. Reading our five books for millions of hours. We ask Thermostat to hot Room all the way up so our everything will dry. We put all our friends back in their right places. Everything has a name and a face, and anything that gets too tired or breaks, we can recycle into something new.

MA: Thanks, Jack.

LITTLE JACK: You're welcome, Ma.

MA: OK, TV time now.

3

He switches it on.

LITTLE JACK: Look, it's the rock star planet.

BIG JACK: Persons in TV are made just of colours, and
sometimes hundreds of them fit together, and sometimes
just one person all big, with clothes instead of skin, and
really red mouths and big eyes with black edges laughing
and shouting. I like the cartoon planet and the police
planet for chasing bad guys and the house-knocker-downer
planet. Houses are like lots of Rooms stuck together,
sometimes the persons go in their outsides and weather
happens to them.

MA: TV off now, or our brains will rot.

He switches it off.

She hands him 'Alice in Wonderland'.

LITTLE JACK: Hi Alice.

BIG JACK: Alice is always trying to get out into the garden but
she's never the right bigness at the right time. I read for
pages and pages till the Cheshire Cat.

LITTLE JACK: *(Reading aloud.)* 'Would you tell me, please, which
way I ought –' *(Pronounces the 'g'.)*

MA: *(Correcting him.)* 'Ought.' It means should.

LITTLE JACK: *(Reading aloud.)* 'Would you tell me, please, which
way I ought to go from here?'

MA: Excellent reading.

She checks her watch, anxious.

A quarter to nine, Grocery List.

BIG JACK: I write out the Groceries in my neatest letters with
none of them backwards.

LITTLE JACK writes each word as MA dictates.

MA: *Please, Pasta, Lentils, Cheese, Grapes, Vitamins, Thanks.* Excellent. Now Bedtime.

LITTLE JACK: And you know what, Ma, tomorrow's going to be my birthday!

MA: I can't believe you'll be five.

LITTLE JACK: Night, Ma.

MA: Three kisses.

LITTLE JACK: Five!

MA: Night, Jack.

COMING ROUND THE MOUNTAIN SONG

MA sings while she breastfeeds LITTLE JACK.

MA: She'll be coming round the mountain
When she comes,
She'll be coming round the mountain
When she comes...

> *She puts him to bed in Wardrobe and shuts the doors.*

BIG JACK: Off to sleep as quick as a blink. Squeeze eyes shut and count twenty teeth and fall down down down.

MA: She'll be driving six white horses
When she comes,
She'll be driving six white horses
When she comes,
She'll be driving six white horses,
She'll be driving six white horses,
She'll be driving six white horses
When she comes.

> *MA scribbles a 'help us' note and hides it in the rubbish bag, which she leaves by Door. Looks at her watch and decides OLD*

5

> *NICK's not coming tonight. She punches random numbers into Keypad.*

We will kill the old red rooster
When she comes,
We will kill the old red rooster
When she comes,
We will kill the old red rooster,
We will kill the old red rooster,
We will kill the old red rooster
When she comes.

> *She lifts Lamp and climbs onto Table, flashing Lamp on and off in an irregular signal for anyone who might see.*

We'll all sing hallelujah
When she comes,
We'll all sing hallelujah
When she comes,
We'll all sing hallelujah,
We'll all sing hallelujah,
We'll all sing hallelujah
When she comes.

> *Giving up, she climbs down and puts Lamp back. She lies down in Bed.*

BIRTHDAY

LITTLE JACK bursts out of Wardrobe.

LITTLE JACK: Ma, I'm five!

MA: Happy birthday.

LITTLE JACK: Tell me the Jack story.

MA: *(Pretending not to understand.)* Hm, Jack the Giant Killer?

LITTLE JACK: No.

MA: Jack and the Beanstalk?

LITTLE JACK: No.

MA: Jack and the Seven-League Boots?

LITTLE JACK: The Jack and Ma story.

MA: Oh, *that* story. OK, here we go. A long long time ago, I was all sad. I cried and cried till I didn't have any tears left. I wouldn't wash and I wouldn't eat and I left TV on all day and nearly turned into a zombie.

BIG JACK: But then you had a good idea –

MA: I started wishing and wishing for you. And you heard me all the way up in Heaven. So I took a deep breath and grew a little bigger…and then a little bit bigger than that… till you were strong enough to zoom down through Outer Space past the Sun and Moon and all the Planets and right through Skylight down down down down down into my tummy.

MA wraps LITTLE JACK up tight.

You were living inside me like yellow crayon on blue makes green. And you grew…

LITTLE JACK: And I grew…

LITTLE JACK starts to grow.

MA: And everything I ate made you bigger, and every song I sang made you braver, till –

LITTLE JACK: I was ready steady go!

MA: I felt you kicking, boom boom, and I said –

LITTLE JACK / BIG JACK / MA: Jack's on his way!

MA: Then you popped out onto Rug with your eyes wide open. There's the stain.

LITTLE JACK: You cut the cord and I was free.

MA produces a page rolled up and tied with a purple ribbon.

MA: Surprise! It's your birthday present.

BIG JACK: That's the ribbon from the thousand chocolates, the time Christmas happened.

MA: Would you like it now or after breakfast?

LITTLE JACK: When are presents meant to open?

MA: Will I choose for you?

LITTLE JACK: I'm five, so *I* have to choose. I choose – now.

MA: Open up. Gently.

LITTLE JACK unrolls and puzzles over the picture.

BIG JACK: It's a drawing, I don't know what it's about and then I turn it and…

BIG JACK / LITTLE JACK: It's me!

BIG JACK: Like in Mirror but more, my head and arm and shoulder in my sleep t-shirt. I was asleep but Ma was awake drawing me.

MA: Blu-Tack, here.

LITTLE JACK: *(Pointing to a wall.)* Here.

MA: *(Shakes her head.)* Maybe inside Wardrobe?

BIG JACK: She doesn't want Old Nick to see. The drawing's a secret surprise present, just for Ma and me. She doesn't like to talk about Old Nick. Mostly she calls him just him. I don't know if he's real like us, or maybe half. He only happens in the night, like bats.

LITTLE JACK sticks the drawing inside Wardrobe.

MA: Time to wash hands.

He does.

And brush teeth.

LITTLE JACK brushes his teeth with the single brush.

BIG JACK: Brush brush brush really hard so the germs don't sneak in a hole when we're not looking and rot our teeth like Ma's Bad Tooth.

MA: Time for vitamins.

MA spills the last vitamin into her hand.

LITTLE JACK: Only one left.

MA: Half for each of us.

She breaks it. Biting down on the vitamin, she feels stabbing pain, rubs her jaw.

LITTLE JACK: Is Bad Tooth bad today?

MA: Mind over matter, mind over matter, if we don't mind –

LITTLE JACK / MA: It doesn't matter!

She takes a painkiller.

LITTLE JACK: I have a bad tooth too.

MA: Oh Jack! Where does it hurt?

He bursts out laughing.

LITTLE JACK: Tricked you.

MA: Not funny.

MA cooks breakfast.

BIG JACK: Ma makes the porridge on the ring of Cooker that goes red. I can't touch because bad idea, if the red ever goes against my t-shirt, there'll be fire, with flames running all over Room and burning us to ashes, coughing and choking and screaming with the worst pain ever.

I play with Labyrinth for millions of hours. Blue Crayon loves to hide in Labyrinth, so I have to shake her sideways and upside-down before he rolls out, whew. Then I send a peanut into Labyrinth on an expedition and a short spaghetti not cooked. Toothbrush guards a tower and squirts out boiling oil on the enemies, ha! Then Eggsnake sneaks up and goes all the way around the enemies and spits poison, double ha!

MA: Time for Breakfast.

They sit down to eat.

BIG JACK: Now I'm five I've got superpowers. I'm going to grow and grow to be a gigantic giant. But not the bad kind.

MA: Look how big your muscles are. Massive.

BIG JACK: Huge. Enormous. Huge-ormous! Excellent word sandwich.

MA: You know what we're going to do now? We're going to bake you a birthday cake.

LITTLE JACK is astonished.

BIG JACK: I never had a birthday cake with candles. Fire burns but candles make it safe because they're magic.

LITTLE JACK and MA make the cake.

Ma says ice cream's just TV but vegetables are real, especially yucky green beans. Lakes and seas are too big to be real, but water's real when it's in Sink or Toilet or Bath. Groceries are just TV, but when Old Nick brings them into Room they turn real. That's the opposite of our poos, because poos are real in Toilet, but then they swim away and I think they turn TV.

MA stops beating the batter, to shake out her sore wrist.

LITTLE JACK takes over, beating the batter.

MA spoons it into the tin.

Trees are too big to be real – only Plant is, but she's small. Cats and horses are just TV, but once there was a mosquito that sucked my blood in the night, she was real till Ma splatted her.

MA puts the tin in Cooker.

Dogs are just TV except my dog Lucky, he might turn real some day if I wish hard enough like Ma wished for me.

MA takes the cake out and produces five smarties.

MA: Five chocolates…

LITTLE JACK is astonished.

I saved them from Sundaytreat one time in the summer. Five in the shape of a number five… Ta-dah!

LITTLE JACK: Now the candles.

MA: Jack – that's what the chocolates are for, to show you're five.

LITTLE JACK: You said a real birthday cake, that means candles.

MA: I'm sorry, I don't have any candles. Want to try your cake?

LITTLE JACK: Stinky cake!

MA: Jack. Taste it.

She cuts it.

Please.

He eats.

LITTLE JACK: That's the yummiest I ever ate.

MA: Happy birthday, Jack.

LITTLE JACK: Next week when I'm six you better ask for candles for Sundaytreat.

MA: Next year, you mean.

Now. Story time. Let's see. Nelson on Robben Island?

LITTLE JACK: Got free after twenty-seven years and became the president.

MA: Princess Diana?

LITTLE JACK: Should have worn her seatbelt.

MA: The Count of Monte Cristo?

LITTLE JACK: He hid in a sack.

MA: That's right, he lay all stiff like a dead body, and the guards threw him in the sea, but he didn't drown.

LITTLE JACK: He wriggled out and swam away, ha!

MA: I think you know all the stories.

LITTLE JACK: One I never had before, please?

MA: Hm. Once upon a time, there's a mermaid sitting on the rocks, combing her hair, when a fisherman sneaks up and catches her in his net.

LITTLE JACK: He thinks she's a fish.

MA: No, he just wants to own her. He takes her to his cottage and he hides her magic comb so she can't go home to her family. Then she has a baby –

LITTLE JACK: Baby Jack?

MA: *(Nods.)* But whenever the fisherman's out fishing she looks around the cottage, and one day she finds her magic comb and runs away to the sea again.

LITTLE JACK: No!

MA: *(Guessing the problem.)* She brings her Baby Jack with her, of course. They're free. And when the fisherman comes back, the cottage is empty and he never sees them again.

LITTLE JACK: Ha. But does he drown?

MA: The fisherman?

LITTLE JACK: Baby Jack?

MA: No no, he's half merman, he can breathe air or water.

LITTLE JACK: Really? Is that a true story?

MA: Well…stories are a different kind of true.

LITTLE JACK: Can I have another?

MA checks her watch.

MA: Nearly nine! Bedtime.

She opens Wardrobe for him.

LITTLE JACK: Ma, do we go in TV for dreaming?

MA: No. We're never anywhere but here.

She kisses him goodnight and shuts Wardrobe's doors.

VISIT FROM OLD NICK

Slow electronic beeps warn of the opening of Door. Sound of heavy Door opening then shutting behind OLD NICK.

MA hangs up his coat and opens him a beer.

BIG JACK: Maybe Door makes Old Nick by magic with the beep beep beep. I never even knew his name till I saw a cartoon about a guy that comes in the night called Old Nick. But our one doesn't look like the TV one with horns and a beard and a tail.

OLD NICK: The grapes were a ridiculous price, so I got a tin of pears.

MA: OK.

BIG JACK: Nothing makes Ma scared except Old Nick. He never sees me but he knows I'm in Wardrobe. Even when I was Baby Jack, Ma wrapped me up in Blanket and hid me away, all the times Old Nick came.

OLD NICK: That a birthday cake? Should've told me, I could've brought the boy a present.

BIG JACK: *Another* present!

OLD NICK: Can I've a slice?

MA: It's getting stale. If you really want...

OLD NICK: No, forget it, you're the boss. I just take out your rubbish, trek around the kidswear section, 'Are You Being Served' madam...

MA: Thanks.

OLD NICK: There, didn't hurt, did it? Like pulling teeth, sometimes.

BIG JACK: I wonder would it hurt if Old Nick looked at me? Maybe I'd turn into stone. Zombies bite and make you undead, vampires suck you till you're floppy, giants dangle you by your legs and munch you up, *be he alive or be he dead I'll grind his bones to make my bread.*

OLD NICK: *(Mouth full.)* Yeah, pretty stale.

SQUEAKING BED SONG

BIG JACK: I wait for his boots to drop. They fall on Floor, one thump, two thumps, that's how I know he's going to get into Bed with Ma now and make it squeak. I count the squeaks because I'm excellent at numbers. I have to count, I can't lose count, if I lose count I don't know what. 1, 2, 3, 4, 5, 6, 7, 8, 9, 10...

    He keeps counting through MA's song.

MA: I am not inside myself.
I am watching someone else.
Half of me's alive
And half is dead.

He will fill me up with blood.
Blood will save me, so will love.
Half of me's alive
And half is dead.

If I save you from him,
You will save me.
I am saving you from him.
You are all that's saving me.

You are why I am alive.
You are why I will survive.
Half of me is dead
And half's alive.

If I save you from him,
You will save me.
I am saving you from him.
You are all that's saving me.

All my bones are reaching for out,
But I can take it.
All my bones are bleeding out,
All the dark I've tasted.

All my bones are reaching for out,
But I can take it.
All my bones are bleeding out,
All the dark I've tasted.

If I save you from him,
You will save me.
I am saving you from him.
You are all that's saving me.

If I save you from him,
You will save me.
I am saving you from him.
You are all that's saving me.

OLD NICK collapses on her.

Then puts his boots back on.

He enters the code on Keypad, covering it with his hand. Door beeps, then lets him out and shuts behind him.

MOUSE

Morning.

LITTLE JACK gets out of Wardrobe.

BIG JACK: Skylight's half dark this morning, she's winking. Oh I remember, that's snow, because it's winter now. TV snow's white, but real snow looks nearly black, that's funny.

LITTLE JACK: Rise and shine, Ma. There's snow.

BIG JACK: Just sometimes Ma has a Gone Day. That's when she won't wake up, she stays in Bed with her head under Pillow and won't talk or give me some or anything.

LITTLE JACK eats cereal.

So I eat cold stuff and watch TV with the sound down low and wait. I wait and wait for zillions of hours and I don't be scared because Ma always gets up sooner or later.

LITTLE JACK turns his head.

It's an alive thing, an animal, for really real not TV, and he's eating crumbs from my birthday cake, and I think what he is is, he's a mouse!

LITTLE JACK approaches Mouse, tentative.

LITTLE JACK: Hello Mouse.

He gently puts down crumbs.

Don't be scared. Please stay. Will you be my friend?

Waking, MA hurls a book across Room, making Mouse flee.

You made him gone!

MA: I had to. He'll steal our food, bring germs in, make us ill...

LITTLE JACK: Mouse wouldn't do that, he promises.

MA: Where there's one, there'll be ten, we'll be overrun.

LITTLE JACK: Why didn't you tell Old Nick it was my birthday?

MA: He's not our friend.

LITTLE JACK: He might have brought me a present. It might have been my dog Lucky turned to real.

MA: We've no room for a dog. *(Hears the word as JACK would, and corrects it.)* No *space*. Dogs need walks.

LITTLE JACK: You and me are always walking.

MA: A dog would drive us nuts in here. Cooped up with the barking, scratching, the germs – eating half our food –

LITTLE JACK: Lucky can have mine, I'm not hungry.

MA: Jack! There is no Lucky, he's not real. You just made him up in your head.

> *LITTLE JACK is crushed.*

Come here. I'm sorry.

> *She hugs him.*

Time for Bed.

> *She breastfeeds him.*

BIG JACK: I wish snow was inside Room, but I suppose it would be really really cold and make us dead, so I wish Sun comes up strong tomorrow and Room's bright again.

VITAMINS

MA puts LITTLE JACK to bed in wardrobe.

BIG JACK: Maybe tonight Old Nick won't come, if I wish and wish and wish. But while I'm wishing I get an idea. I think maybe Old Nick lives in TV. All the time he's not here, he's getting our groceries in shops, and shops are TV so he must be TV too. But then how come we never see him, all the times we're watching?

> *Three beeps. Sound of heavy Door opening. Door shuts. OLD NICK comes in with groceries.*

OLD NICK: Hi.

MA: Hi.

BIG JACK: I'm not allowed to get out of Wardrobe, not any part of me.

> *She hangs up his coat and opens him a beer.*

MA: I was wondering, is there any chance, if it might be possible to clear some of the snow off the skylight sometime? It's only that it makes it dark in here. Darker.

OLD NICK: Yeah, great idea. Let's get all the neighbours looking out their windows, wondering why I'm up a ladder scraping snow off the roof of my shed.

MA: Oh. I didn't think.

OLD NICK: It's not your strong suit.

MA: I shouldn't have bothered you. Everything's fine.

OLD NICK: All right then.

> *Putting the groceries away, MA notices what's missing.*

MA: Did you not buy the vitamins?

OLD NICK: Those things are a waste of money, they go straight down the toilet.

MA: Maybe if we had a better diet…

OLD NICK: Here we go again.

MA: We're cheaper to keep than a dog. We don't even have shoes.

OLD NICK: You have no idea how good you've got it here. Above ground, natural light, air conditioning. Fresh fruit, toiletries, click your fingers and it's there. Plenty of girls would be down on bended knees saying thanks for a setup like this. Especially with the kid. No drunk drivers to worry about, drug pushers, perverts… And how do you expect me to keep paying for everything?

MA: What do you mean?

OLD NICK: You know nothing about the world of today.

MA: Has something happened?

OLD NICK: Three months I've been laid off, and have you had to worry your pretty little head?

MA: Are you looking for another job?

OLD NICK: There are no jobs, so shut your mouth!

His roar makes LITTLE JACK let out a gasp.

It speaks.

MA: He's asleep.

OLD NICK: I don't think so. You keep him shut in there all day as well as all night?

MA: Of course not.

OLD NICK: Some mother you are. Little freak's got two heads or something?

MA: He's fine.

OLD NICK: Hey Jack, want to come out and say hi?

19

MA: Come to bed.

OLD NICK: Think I've got a lollipop somewhere. I bet you'll like it. I know boys, I was one once.

MA: Come to bed. Please!

She brings him to Bed.

OUT OF WARDROBE

BIG JACK: I wake up and it's still night. I wait for hours and hours. I can't switch off, and the more I try the wakier I get.

LITTLE JACK opens Wardrobe.

Not a foot, not a face, not even a finger, not while Old Nick's here. But he's asleep and Ma's asleep, nobody sees me climbing out. I just want to see the lollipop. What colour is it? Are there colours in the dark?

LITTLE JACK creeps over to Bed.

A boot. A giant boot. I never saw Old Nick near. Huge. Near and huge, nuge. I'm just going to peek one time to see if he's a real human like us. His face is all white, I think it's made of rock. I put my finger out, not to touch, just nearly.

OLD NICK wakes.

OLD NICK: Hey, boy.

MA wakes, panics and lashes out.

MA: Get away from him! Get away from him!

LITTLE JACK flees back to Wardrobe.

OLD NICK chokes MA.

OLD NICK: Stop that noise.

Then he lets go.

MA: *(Hoarse.)* Just leave Jack alone. It's all I've ever asked.

OLD NICK: You ask for stuff every time I open the door.

He taps the code into Keypad.

MA: It's all for Jack.

OLD NICK: Just don't forget where you got him.

Door beeps. He pulls on his boots and coat. Door opens then shuts behind him.

MA: Jack?

She rushes to Wardrobe.

LITTLE JACK: I'm sorry!

MA: It's OK, it's OK. Everything's hunky-dory.

LITTLE JACK: Why did Old Nick call me a little freak? Is something wrong about me?

MA: No!

LITTLE JACK: Why did he say don't forget where you got me? Wasn't it Heaven?

MA: He thinks you're his – he meant, don't forget who you belong to.

LITTLE JACK: But I belong to you.

She hugs him.

POWER CUT

BIG JACK: I wake up and see smoke coming out my mouth.

Waking up in Bed with MA, LITTLE JACK shivers and huffs his breath.

LITTLE JACK: Ma. Rise and shine. We're dragons.

Groggy, MA realises the heat has been switched off.

Tries Lamp: nothing.

MA: He's cut the power.

With wild hope she tries Door. Then, just to be sure, Thermostat, Cooker, Fridge.

LITTLE JACK tries TV.

BIG JACK: The Planets are gone.

MA: We need to wear double clothes today and keep moving, moving, moving, to stay warm till he turns the power back on, OK?

LITTLE JACK: OK.

They run on the spot, do jumping jacks, dance, jump...

BIG JACK: We do all our movings for hundreds of hours. I'm tired but I'm still cold, coldy-tired, colired.

LITTLE JACK: When's he going to turn the power back on?

MA: Soon. As soon as he's not cross with us anymore. *(Corrects herself.)* Cross with me.

She flops down in a square of light under Skylight.

LITTLE JACK joins her.

LITTLE JACK: Sun's still on.

MA: Yeah, he can't turn off the Sun.

BIG JACK: Maybe he tried but he couldn't. Maybe he burned his fingers, ha!

MA: Hey, we forgot to do Scream.

SCREAM SONG

MA and LITTLE JACK get onto Table.

BIG JACK: We Scream every day but not Saturdays or Sundays because we're not allowed to be noisy then. Ma and me climb up because Skylight's thinner than Walls so she lets our sound burst out into Outer Space. We bring things for extra noisiness. We hold hands not to fall and clear our throats.

MA: Ready?

BIG JACK: Steady?

MA / LITTLE JACK: Go!

> *They scream. Then stop to take a breath. They listen.*

MA: Under the bolt of the grain
And held in the mouth of the sun,
Cold in the light of the day,
We are the light,
We are the light,
We are the light.
And underground baby is safe,
And underground baby is sound.
We are the light,
We are the lost,
We are not found.

And my bones you break,
And my heart you ate,
And your soul will burn,
But my son will learn.

Under the bolt of the grain
And held in the mouth of the sun,
Cold in the light of the day,
We are the light,
We are the light,

23

We are the light.
And underground baby is safe,
And underground baby is sound.
We are the light,
We are the lost,
We are not found.

And my bones you break,
And my heart you ate,
And your soul will burn,
But my son will learn.

And my bones you break,
And my heart you ate,
And your soul will burn,
But my son will learn.

LITTLE JACK: Why don't the aliens ever shout back?

MA: I suppose they still can't hear us.

LITTLE JACK: When we do Scream tomorrow we'll be double
   loud.

> *They get down from Table.*

ALICE

Light fades. LITTLE JACK and MA eat a meagre, cold meal.

BIG JACK: Dark's getting in everywhere.

LITTLE JACK: I don't like it.

MA: It's OK. We know each other without looking, don't we?

> *MA bites, flinches. Reaches into her mouth and takes out a
> rotten tooth.*

LITTLE JACK: Is that Bad Tooth?

MA: Better out than in. He can't hurt me anymore.

LITTLE JACK marvels at it.

LITTLE JACK: A bit of you.

MA: Not any more.

LITTLE JACK: Still.

He closes his hand around the tooth, hoarding the treasure.

MA shivers, rubbing her arms.

MA: Are you cold?

LITTLE JACK: When's Old Nick going to uncut the power?

MA: Soon.

LITTLE JACK: When soon?

MA: I don't know.

LITTLE JACK: *(Alarmed.)* Yeah you do, you know everything.

MA: I know he can't stop the Sun coming up tomorrow.

LITTLE JACK: It's a long time till tomorrow.

MA: Jack, would you like a story?

LITTLE JACK: Yeah.

MA: I have a new one for you. Now you're a big boy, I think you're ready for a big story. Are you ready?

LITTLE JACK nods.

I haven't always been in Room. Remember Alice, before she fell down the rabbit hole?

He nods.

Well, I was a little girl like Alice.

He shakes his head.

I lived with my mum and dad, you'd call them Gran and Grandad.

BIG JACK: A mum like on TV?

MA: They wished and wished for me like I did for you. We lived in a house in the world.

LITTLE JACK shakes his head.

BIG JACK: But Ma can't be a little girl. She's in Room with me. Why's she pretending, is it a game I don't know?

MA: There's a whole world on the other side of these walls, just out there, just that much away. *(Shows distance with her hands.)* Mountains and lakes and skyscrapers, trees and cars and skateboards and cats and dogs and playgrounds and the house where I was a little girl with my mum and dad.

BIG JACK: There's no Gran and Grandad and mountains and stuff and everything. I never heard such a stupid story.

MA picks up LITTLE JACK's homemade planet earth.

MA: See, Room's right here, in a city in a country in a continent on Earth.

BIG JACK: *On* Earth? That's ridiculous – Earth's up there spinning around with all the other Planets.

MA: Me and my mum and dad, we used to swing in the hammock behind our house and eat ice cream.

BIG JACK: Ice cream's only TV.

MA: What you and me see on TV, that's pictures of real things that are here on Earth, just outside these walls.

LITTLE JACK: Where would they all fit?

MA: They just do, there's room for everything, you wouldn't believe how big the world is. How beautiful.

BIG JACK: I'm staring and staring up at Skylight till my eyes hurt but all I see through her is sky. There's nothing like ships or buses or girls or horses or anything Ma said.

BIG JACK /LITTLE JACK: Liar liar pants on fire!

MA: No, I had to kind of lie to you before, Jack, because you were too small to understand, but now you're five, it's the opposite of lying, I'm unlying.

LITTLE JACK: I'm hungry.

MA: There's another part to my story.

LITTLE JACK: I want a different story.

MA: Let me finish this one. I was a little girl and then a big girl and then I was nearly grown up. One day, seven years ago, Old Nick stole me. Do you understand, Jack? He told me his dog was ill, he tricked me into his truck.

LITTLE JACK: What's the dog's name?

MA: There was no dog, it was all a trick. I woke up in his shed.

LITTLE JACK: Why?

MA: He wanted to own me. Be the boss of everything. D'you see now, Jack? Room's the shed. I can't open Door because I don't know the numbers. For seven years I've been trying. Seven years I've been locked in this stinking little room.

LITTLE JACK throws the earth away.

LITTLE JACK / BIG JACK: Blah blah blah blah blah, I don't believe in your stinky world.

MA gathers him into her arms. He resists, then slumps into her embrace.

POWER BACK ON

LITTLE JACK and MA sleep curled up together. The light snaps on, waking him.

BIG JACK: Lamp's awake. All the power's back. Everything's hunky-dory.

LITTLE JACK: Morning Room. Morning Walls, Wardrobe, Skylight.

MA: Jack.

LITTLE JACK: Morning Plant, Morning Labyrinth –

MA: Jack! Stop that and listen to me.

LITTLE JACK: I want to watch TV.

MA: D'you remember what I told you yesterday?

LITTLE JACK: TV, TV, TV!

MA: All right, all right.

> *LITTLE JACK turns on TV and loses himself in what he sees.*

BIG JACK: How can TV be pictures of real things? And how can TV persons stand up when they're so flat? And if there's rivers and lakes and seas whizzing around out there, wouldn't they wet everything? But Ma said it's real. Persons too, women and men and babies and teachers and burglars, they're all walking and bicycling and skateboarding around in the world just outside Walls, everyone's out there but us. Are we the only ones not in the world?

> *LITTLE JACK turns off TV without being asked.*

LITTLE JACK: Old Nick shouldn't have stolen you, that's not allowed.

MA: You believe me!

LITTLE JACK: What about we push Wardrobe so she blocks Door and Old Nick can't come in, ha!

MA: But then we wouldn't have any food anymore, would we?

BIG JACK: What about we wait till he comes in, and we kick him and bash him and smash him!

LITTLE JACK: Kill him dead!

MA: But then we'd never know the code, would we? We'd get
   hungrier and hungrier till we died. Before you were born,
   I scared him with Zigzag Knife so he'd tell me the secret
   code, but he broke my wrist – that's why it's bad now. Old
   Nick doesn't matter. What matters is, we need to get out.

LITTLE JACK: *(Alarmed.)* Out in the world?

MA: All these years, Jack, that's what I've wanted for us. In the
   beginning I prayed for your Grandad and Gran to come
   rescue us, but they don't know where we are, you see:
   Room's not on any map.

LITTLE JACK: Why don't you like it here with me?

MA: Oh Jack. I always like being with you.

LITTLE JACK: You said Room's stinky.

MA: I want to be with you, but outside.

LITTLE JACK: Bad idea.

MA: It's a good idea, the best idea.

LITTLE JACK: Dumbo Ma.

MA: You don't know what you're missing.

BIG JACK: Ma doesn't know everything there is.

MA: All these years, I've been flashing Lamp every night, but
   nobody ever notices. I hide a note in every bag of rubbish
   but nobody finds them. When we do Scream, nobody
   hears. You know what, Jack? We're going to have to rescue
   ourselves.

LITTLE JACK: How?

MA: I have a plan. D'you want to hear it?

PLAN A

Later, night.

BIG JACK: We're going to trick Old Nick, just like Jack in the stories is always tricking the Giant. But it's such a tricky trick, Ma has to keep explaining it.

> *LITTLE JACK's in Bed. MA presses a really hot wet flannel to his face.*

LITTLE JACK: Ow!

MA: The hot water's to make your face hot and red like you have a fever, because you got so cold when he cut the power.

BIG JACK: How can cold make me hot?

MA: Trust me, we're going to pretend so well that Old Nick will believe us. Play that you're really ill, but play for real, no laughing.

LITTLE JACK: I don't know how to be ill.

MA: Just stay all floppy and I'll be all worried.

> *She uses her fingers to make herself retch on the pillow.*

LITTLE JACK: Stop!

MA: Sorry, you need to smell as if you've been sick. Old Nick needs to think you're really ill so he'll take you in his truck to the hospital. And the minute you get there, you'll say to the doctor, "Help, help!"

LITTLE JACK: *You* can say to the doctor.

MA: I'll still be here in Room.

BIG JACK: Bad idea.

> *LITTLE JACK shakes his head.*

MA: He'll never bring us both. You can do it, Jack. You've got your superpowers. You'll rescue me and we'll be free.

Door beeps.

(To LITTLE JACK.) Sh!

She hides the hot flannel.

Door opens and OLD NICK comes in.

Jack's ill!

Door shuts.

OLD NICK: You know the drill – not a peep out of you till the door's shut.

MA: Sorry, it's just – he got so cold, when you cut the power. He woke up with chills, and now he's burning up...

OLD NICK: Give him one of those tablets.

MA: I've been trying all day, but he sicks them back up.

OLD NICK moves towards LITTLE JACK.

MA: Don't.

OLD NICK: Let me feel him.

He touches LITTLE JACK's hot face. LITTLE JACK whimpers and squirms away.

I'll bring him something stronger. Antibiotics.

MA: He's five years old! He could go into convulsions.

OLD NICK: Hysterics won't help.

MA: He needs to go to A&E.

OLD NICK: They'd ask questions.

MA: Just tell them he's a lost child, you don't know his name.

OLD NICK: It's too risky.

MA: Please.

OLD NICK: Get off me.

He shoves her aside and taps the code into Keypad.

MA: Please.

Beeps.

I'm begging you!

Door opens and lets him out. Thud of Door shutting.

GOD SENT ME THE DEVIL SONG

Later. LITTLE JACK is sleeping.

MA: God sent me the devil,
    Made myself his whore.
    God sent you to save me,
    Knew I'd love you more.

    You, my warm and water,
    And all I cannot tell.
    You and I have waited
    Too long in this hell.

    God won't save me,
    Or my baby.
    My bones broken,
    Still I'm ready.

    I can see the light.
    I can see it.
    Need to breathe in, and
    I can see the light.
    I can see it.
    Need to breathe in, and
    You will be the light.
    We need to take it,
    This chance of making it
    Out into the light.

This life or death of us
Is all that's left for us.

God sent me the devil,
Made myself his whore.

God you're telling me
To gamble my baby.
God you're forcing me
To use my baby.
God you're testing me
To risk my baby.
God you can take me,
Please, just save my baby.

God sent me the devil.

PLAN B

Next day.

MA: Jack! Listen to me.

LITTLE JACK: I'm sick of listening to you.

MA: Plan A didn't work because Old Nick was too mean to take you to the hospital. So this is Plan B: this time you're going to be dead.

LITTLE JACK: I don't want to be dead.

MA: Only pretending. Like the Count of Monte Cristo, remember? But we don't have a sack so I'm going to roll you up in Rug the second we hear Door beep. You won't move a muscle, remember? You'll be playing dead.

LITTLE JACK: Let's play something else.

MA: This isn't a game. Where's Bad Tooth?

> *LITTLE JACK points to his gum.*

See, you've got a bit of me always with you. Old Nick will carry you out, rolled up in Rug...

BIG JACK: What if he unwraps me?

MA: He'll put you in his pickup truck to *(stops herself from saying 'bury')* bring you somewhere else. And as soon as you feel the engine turn on – vroom – that means he's too busy driving to look back, so that's when you come alive again and start wriggling out of Rug. You're good at remembering, aren't you? Dead, Truck, Wriggle Out. Then when the truck slows down at the stop sign, you'll Jump, Run to Somebody...

BIG JACK: Who's Somebody?

MA: The first person you see on the street.

LITTLE JACK: Not Old Nick.

MA: Anybody but him.

LITTLE JACK: An actual TV person.

MA: They're not...they're as real as you and me, Jack. It's not TV, it's the world, remember?

LITTLE JACK / BIG JACK: I can't remember all of it.

MA: You'll give the Somebody the Note.

BIG JACK: The Somebody can read.

MA: And they'll call the Police, and the Police will... *(She's uncertain about this.)* Look in all the back gardens till they find Room. Then they'll break Door open and you'll rescue me. So: Dead, Truck, Wriggle Out, Jump, Run to Somebody, Give the Note, Police, Rescue Ma. That's our Plan B. OK? Say it. Dead...

BIG JACK / LITTLE JACK: Dead, Truck, Jump...

MA: Wriggle Out, *then* Jump, Run...

BIG JACK / LITTLE JACK: Run to Somebody, Police...

MA: Give the Note, *then* Police. Are you scared? Me too. Scared is what we're feeling but brave is what we're doing. Scaredy-brave.

LITTLE JACK: Scave.

MA: Good word sandwich.

She checks her watch, nervous.

When you're in Rug, you mustn't move and you mustn't make a sound, because then Old Nick will guess you're alive and he'll…get really angry. Let's practise rolling you up.

LITTLE JACK: No!

MA: Try keeping your arms like this *(Crosses his arms on his chest, sticking his elbows out.)* so there's more room inside Rug.

MA and LITTLE JACK rehearse.

BIG JACK: But Room's not inside Rug, it's Rug that's inside Room, and I'm inside Rug tight tight like I was inside Ma before I was born, but this time I'm stuck, I'm kicking and kicking but I can't pop out.

LITTLE JACK: I want a different plan. What's Plan C?

MA: There aren't any more after B.

LITTLE JACK breaks away from MA.

BIG JACK: But I have a plan, it's the best plan.

LITTLE JACK: Let's just stay.

BIG JACK: Room is where we live, with all our friends.

MA: Oh Jack. It's too small.

LITTLE JACK: No it's not.

BIG JACK: It's the same as always.

LITTLE JACK spins freely to prove he has enough space. But MA catches him in her arms.

MA: I'm your Ma. That means sometimes I choose for both of us.

She tries to put him back into Rug.

He resists.

LITTLE JACK / BIG JACK: I hate you!

She's thrown, for a moment.

MA: That's all right. I brought you into Room. I didn't mean to, but I've never once been sorry. And now it's my job to get you out. It has to be tonight, Jack.

LITTLE JACK: Why?

MA: Because Old Nick cut the power. And yeah, he turned it back on, but what if he doesn't, next time? Who knows what he'll do to us? If he was even half human he'd have brought you to the hospital. You know your heart?

LITTLE JACK: Bam bam bam.

MA: No, but your feeling bit, where you're sad or scared or laughing? Well, Old Nick hasn't got a feeling bit.

LITTLE JACK: What's he got instead?

MA: Just a gap. So we have to get ourselves out of Room, and it has to be tonight.

LITTLE JACK: Maybe when I'm six.

MA: Tonight.

She checks her watch again.

Time to get back in Rug.

Miserable, LITTLE JACK lies down. She rolls him up.

Remember, I'll be playing that I'm crying and crying because you're dead. I'll pretend I don't want him to take you away. But really I'll be cheering you on. You'll hear me

singing in your head, Jack, all the way out into the world.
We're scave, aren't we? We're so scave.

LITTLE JACK: Ma.

MA: What is it?

LITTLE JACK: Bye-bye.

She pats him through Rug. Waits. Sings one wobbly line:

MA: She'll be coming round the mountain
When she comes,
She'll be coming round –

> *Door beeps. MA stiffens, and puts herself between Little-Jack-in-Rug and Door.*
>
> *Door opens, letting in OLD NICK, and shutting behind him. He does a double-take.*

OLD NICK: What have you got him wrapped up in that for?

MA: He wouldn't wake up.

OLD NICK: Are you sure?

MA: Am I *sure?*

OLD NICK: Ah, you poor girl.

> *He shows the antibiotics.*

It must have been something pretty bad, the tablets
wouldn't have worked anyway.

MA: You killed my baby.

OLD NICK: I did nothing.

> *MA weeps over LITTLE JACK in Rug. OLD NICK waits.*

You can't keep him here, you know.

> *MA holds Rug protectively.*

It's not healthy.

He moves towards her.

MA: No!

OLD NICK: Let me take him.

MA: Not yet.

OLD NICK: I'll give you a minute.

MA: And not in the garden, not this time. If you put him there, I'll hear him crying in the night and I'll tear the place apart, I'll never be quiet again.

OLD NICK: OK, OK.

MA: Promise me!

OLD NICE: I promise, somewhere else, somewhere nice.

MA: With trees.

OLD NICE: Big trees. I'll keep him all wrapped up nice and cosy.

MA: Don't you dare look at him with your filthy eyes. Swear it.

OLD NICK: I swear.

> *He taps the code into Keypad. He scoops up Rug into his arms. Then turns stern, to make sure she doesn't try anything.*

Now get back against the wall.

> *Door beeps. Then opens.*

MA: Jack, Jack, Jack!

> *OLD NICK exits. Door shuts.*

RUN JACK RUN SONG

MA: Dead, truck, wriggle out,
Jump, run, somebody,
Give a note,

38

Police.

Dead, truck, wriggle out,
Jump, run, somebody,
Give a note,
Police.

Run Jack, run Jack, run Jack, run Jack,
Run Jack, run Jack, run Jack, run Jack,
Run Jack, run Jack, run Jack, run Jack,
Run Jack, run Jack, run Jack, run Jack.

And if you don't make it back to me
You'll see Outer Space,
And all your friends from inside the TV
Will be there to keep you safe.

And I will always be in you,
'Cos you are made from me.
Our thoughts are shared,
Mine jump into yours,
Like yellow crayon on blue,
We make green,
Like yellow crayon on blue,
We make green.

Run Jack, run Jack, run Jack, run Jack,
Run Jack, run Jack, run Jack, run Jack,
Run Jack, run Jack, run Jack, run Jack,
Run Jack, run Jack, run Jack, run Jack...

POLICE: *(V.O.)* What's your name? Can you tell me your
name? Can you tell me how old you are? Where do you
live? Where's your Ma right now? In a room, which room?
The man with the truck, was that your dad? Disturbed
minor, possibly a domestic. Jack, would you like a ride in
our police car? Suspect's white male, forties, fifties, fled
the scene in a maroon or dark brown truck. What made
the truck slow down, Jack? You jumped out at the first

39

stop sign? That's a big help. Jack, the room your Ma's in,
is it in a house with stairs or a bungalow? It's not a house?
In a garden. It's a shed? Check satellite for properties
with garden sheds. Any freestanding rear structure with a
skylight.

ACT TWO

POLICE STATION / HOSPITAL

BIG JACK: It's a thousand per cent bright and too loud. The floor's all shiny hard, not like Floor, and the walls are blue and more of them, and persons everywhere not friends of ours.

MA holds LITTLE JACK.

POLICE: Do you recollect the date of the abduction? What about the incident in which your wrist was broken?

MA puts her ear down to LITTLE JACK's mouth.

BIG JACK: Are we bad guys? No, Old Nick is the bad guy.

A DOCTOR in a medical mask replaces the POLICE. We're in a hospital cubicle.

LITTLE JACK: Argh, he doesn't have a face!

BIG JACK: He's sticking out his hand, and Ma does his hand up and down like persons on TV.

DOCTOR: Hello Jack. This is a hospital. You've been a very brave young man.

BIG JACK: That's me he's looking at. But he doesn't know me. Why does he say I'm a man?

LITTLE JACK: *(To MA.)* Are we ill for real or just pretend?

MA: No, this is just a place to stay till we're better.

LITTLE JACK: Better than who?

This confuses LITTLE JACK.

It's the police station again.

POLICE: On roughly how many occasions, would you say? So these assaults were nightly?

BIG JACK: People keep calling Ma different names, not Ma.

MA: I suppose you'll have the same second name, so people won't think you're a different boy called Jack.

LITTLE JACK: *(Troubled.)* What different boy called Jack?

MA: There's millions of boys in the world.

It's the hospital again.

DOCTOR: *(To LITTLE JACK, pointing to his own mask.)* This mask is to keep you safe from any germs floating around that you never met before.

BIG JACK: I thought germs were only in Room, I didn't know the world was full of them too.

LITTLE JACK: *(To MA.)* Are we dying?

The DOCTOR holds out two masks. MA is reluctant.

DOCTOR: Your son's effectively a newborn.

MA fits one mask on herself and one on LITTLE JACK.

It's the police station again.

POLICE: Did the assaults involve violence? So just to be clear, on every single occasion it was non-consensual?

BIG JACK: Old Nick zoomed off in his truck. Now he's not in Room and he's not in the world, my head's worn out from wondering.

LITTLE JACK: I want some now.

He tries to lift MA's shirt, but she doesn't let him.

Hospital again.

MA: *(To DOCTOR.)* When can we see our family?

DOCTOR: I suggest you take things slowly. Re-entry to the world is…

MA: *(Interrupts.)* We're not astronauts!

DOCTOR: You're both going to need detailed blood work, bone density scans, psychiatric assessment… I'd expect challenges in focal distance, spatial orientation, sensory overload…social adjustment, obviously.

MA: Nothing happened to Jack. I kept him safe.

DOCTOR: The key is, you got him out while he's still plastic.

LITTLE JACK: *(To MA.)* No I'm not.

MA: You're not what?

LITTLE JACK: Plastic. I'm real.

> *She hugs him to her.*

> *Police station again.*

POLICE: As a priority we have to go over your allegations in more detail.

MA: Allegations?

POLICE: I'm sorry.

> *MA rocks LITTLE JACK.*

> *Hospital again.*

DOCTOR: We're going to take a look at your mum in a room across the hall there.

MA: No, Jack stays with me.

DOCTOR: We need samples for evidence: blood, urine, hair, fingernail scrapings…

BIG JACK: I don't want them to take Ma's hair and fingernails.

MA: *(To LITTLE JACK.)* You stay here, I'm just going in there.

LITTLE JACK: No! I don't want to be in the world without you.

MA: Just for a minute.

> *She glimpses a screen: relief.*

Look, there's a TV, want to watch?

> *LITTLE JACK perks up at the sight of the TV.*

BIG JACK: It's not our TV in Room but it shows the planets. I'm watching a news planet, mostly blah-blah-blah. But then the most amazing thing, it's me and Ma, Ma carrying me. Us, only different.

TV NEWS: Early reports say that this innocuous shed in a suburban back garden was converted into an impregnable twenty-first-century dungeon by its owner, a bachelor loner according to neighbours. He is still at large and is urgently wanted for questioning. Charges of kidnapping, confinement, sexual assault and battery are expected to be laid.

LITTLE JACK: Ma!

TV NEWS: The two victims, a woman and a small boy, rescued earlier this evening by police, appear to be in a borderline catatonic state after the long nightmare of their captivity. The malnourished, possibly feral child, seemingly unable to walk, has been dubbed the Bonsai Boy. Experts cannot yet agree what kind or degree of longterm damage mother and child may have sustained.

LITTLE JACK: Ma! Us on TV!

> *MA hurries back...*

> *But now she's holding him down so DOCTOR can inject him. LITTLE JACK screams.*

MA: All done. You were so scave.

> *DOCTOR offers a lollipop, but LITTLE JACK ignores it.*

LITTLE JACK: *(To MA.)* Bed!

MA: Just hang on a bit longer and they'll find us somewhere to sleep.

LITTLE JACK: No, but *Bed*, in Room. I've seen the world and I'm tired now.

MA: Oh Jack. Don't you get it? We're never going back to Room.

REUNION

A curtain opens, revealing GRAN waiting.

BIG JACK: There's *another* person with tears coming out all black and her mouth is blood colour like women in TV.

MA: Mum!

GRAN: My baby.

> *MA rips down her mask as she runs to embrace her mother.*

BIG JACK: But Ma's not a baby, she's Ma. I never saw her hug a someone else before. They're hugging for hundreds of hours like Ma doesn't even remember I'm here.

GRAN: My girl. My girl.

MA: Oh Mum. Where's Dad?

GRAN: He's on his way. I always believed, I never gave up.

> *GRAN looks past MA at LITTLE JACK.*

MA: Jack, this is your Gran.

> *MA pulls down his mask to show his face. LITTLE JACK pulls it up again.*

GRAN: Hello Jack. Do you know the word 'hello'?

LITTLE JACK: *(Evading her eyes.)* I know all the words.

GRAN: What a treasure. *(To MA.)* He's the dead spit of you.

LITTLE JACK: *(Alarmed.)* I'm not dead spit.

45

GRAN: Who's a lovely big boy?

The question confuses him. GRAN approaches, but he hides.

MA: He's very affectionate, he's just not used to anyone but me.

GRAN: Of course, of course, no rush, easy does it.

THE FIRST BABY

Later. MA changes herself and LITTLE JACK into new clothes and shoes.

BIG JACK: We're meant to be getting better here in the Hospital. But actually we were better in Room. There weren't any needles stabbing us, or persons talking too loud from all directions or the air changing hotness and coldness and blowiness. Room wasn't too small, it went all the way in every direction. Everything was in its place and every day was just long enough for everything we had to do.

MA flings clothes into the bin.

LITTLE JACK: That's waste.

MA: I don't want anything from that place.

LITTLE JACK: What place?

MA: Room.

She throws away her watch.

LITTLE JACK: Who's the first baby?

MA: What?

LITTLE JACK: You said to the Police about the first baby.

MA: Before you, I had a girl baby. Your sister.

LITTLE JACK: What's her name?

MA: She never got to have a name. Remember the cord?

BIG JACK: You cut the cord and I was free.

MA: Well, hers got tangled around her neck when she was coming out, so she couldn't breathe.

LITTLE JACK: I don't like this story.

MA: Me neither, but let me finish it. Old Nick didn't help, he didn't do a thing. So she came out blue.

LITTLE JACK: Blue?

MA: She never opened her eyes.

LITTLE JACK: Did you cut the cord and she was free?

MA: *(Nods.)* He buried her in the garden, beside Room. Just her body. The rest of her went back up to Heaven.

LITTLE JACK: She got recycled?

> *MA nods.*

When are the Police going to catch him?

MA: Soon.

LITTLE JACK: When is soon?

MA: Forget about him.

> *LITTLE JACK makes an effort.*

BIG JACK: I can't.

MA: Mind over matter.

LITTLE JACK: *(Struggling to believe it.)* If we don't mind –

LITTLE JACK / BIG JACK: He doesn't matter.

MA: You know where we're going?

LITTLE JACK: Room?

MA: No! Home. We're going home.

HOME

A crowd shrieks: 'Welcome home', Congratulations', 'Jack', We love you'.

GRAN lets MA and LITTLE JACK into the house.

MA: Oh Mum.

GRAN: You're OK now. Home safe.

MA: It's all unreal.

GRAN: *(To LITTLE JACK.)* This is your new house. And your
Ma's old house. Isn't that funny?

> *He wanders to the window.*

MA: Who are those nutcases out there?

GRAN: Just well-wishers, glad you're free.

MA: Come away from the window, Jack!

GRAN: They'll take your picture, put you on the Internet.

LITTLE JACK: *(To MA.)* Where's the hammock?

GRAN: Oh, we took that down years ago, when... Now, what
would you like? Milk, juice, we've got orange juice, and
apple, all sorts, the fridge is full to bursting, the neighbours
have been so kind. Thirsty, Jack?

LITTLE JACK: I want some.

GRAN: You want some what? We've got everything.

MA: *(To JACK.)* Not right now. *(To GRAN.)* Isn't Dad here?

GRAN: He's getting on a plane, he won't be long.

> *MA looks at her with suspicion.*

There's been a lot of water under the bridge, since you've
been gone.

MA: No!

GRAN: We stayed together as long as we could.

MA: But why?

GRAN: The not knowing… Your Dad took it very hard. Before he left, he had a funeral.

MA: A funeral?

GRAN: He thought you were…you know.

MA: Couldn't he have waited?

GRAN: Seven years, love.

MA: I know it was seven years. I counted every day of them!

> *MA takes LITTLE JACK by the hand and flees to her room. He's never encountered stairs, but manages to scramble up.*

TWO DAYS AND A HALF

BIG JACK: We've been in the world for two days and a half, it's pretty tricky. Nothing happens when I think it's going to, the times are jumbled up. Like, the rule in Room was 'Bath before Bed' but Ma says there aren't any rules now. I think there are, I just don't know them. In the world, Bath's called Shower and it's from up high crashing down wet on top of our heads. Stairs are like a floor but broken so my feet fall. Windows are like Skylight but sideways with all things showing. I've seen seagulls and motorbikes and persons with sticks in their mouths on fire, and the Moon but cut small. Manners means not making persons cranky. The Gran and the Grandad don't live in the home house in the same bit of the Earth anymore, that's called divorce and Ma cried.

There's strawberries and bacon and ice cream that hurts my head like hitting inside. My poo's hard to push out. The Gran says my tummy will settle down, it's early days yet. Sounds come from places I don't know which and I can't tell who's talking all at the same time. I can't get to sleep not in Wardrobe, the world's too big. When I was four I only knew small things, but now I'm five I know so many big things, they hurt my head.

LITTLE JACK: Ma. Rise and shine.

MA: It's the middle of the night.

LITTLE JACK: Still.

MA: I can't sleep either.

LITTLE JACK: Is this what free is?

MA: Yeah.

LITTLE JACK: How long do we have to stay?

MA: In this house?

LITTLE JACK: In the world, on Planet Earth.

MA: This is where we live now, Jack. Never anywhere but here.

LITTLE JACK: For ever and ever till we die?

    MA nods.

MA: You want some?

    She feeds him.

BIG JACK: No one's in Room, just things. Everything is lying extra still, dust falling, because Ma and me are here.

COFFEE

GRAN: Coffee's in the pot!

    MA and LITTLE JACK come downstairs. GRAN pours juice for JACK, coffee for MA.

MA: Proper coffee!

GRAN: Milk and two sugars, I remember.

MA: Just black, actually.

GRAN: Oh. Didn't he give you milk, even? Or did you keep it all for the boy?

MA doesn't answer. The women sit and drink, stiffly.

LITTLE JACK roots in the bin.

Leave that, sweetie, it's dirty.

MA: Don't touch, Jack.

LITTLE JACK: *(Finding the inside of a toilet roll.)* Can I draw?

GRAN: Not on that!

MA: Use one of your new colouring books.

GRAN: Aren't you coming to have your juice?

MA: Right now, Jack.

GRAN: Oh, there's no hurry. We've all the time in the world.

LITTLE JACK drinks fast.

Slow down or you'll choke.

BIG JACK: All the time in the world? In the world, all the time's mixed up.

LITTLE JACK sips very slowly.

MA: Want one of your new books?

He shakes his head.

GRAN: *(To MA.)* He's such a reader! You didn't get the hang of it till you were seven.

LITTLE JACK: *(To MA.)* Can we do Laundry?

GRAN: Aren't you a love! But there's no need, it's all in the dryer.

LITTLE JACK: *(To MA.)* When's Sundaytreat?

GRAN: It's Wednesday.

MA: You can have a treat any day. What do you want?

LITTLE JACK shrugs.

LITTLE JACK: Is today the day for Cleaning?

GRAN: Why don't you just chill and play with all your new toys?

LITTLE JACK: *(To MA.)* What's chill?

MA: Relax, take it easy, Gran's saying.

LITTLE JACK: What does relax mean?

MA: Not doing anything!

LITTLE JACK tries the hum game, humming 'Swing Low'.

GRAN: Good humming. Do you know how to whistle?

He ignores her and hums another tune at MA, 'She'll be Coming Round the Mountain'.

GRAN whistles the same tune – which intrigues LITTLE JACK, but he keeps working on MA.

LITTLE JACK: Ma. Flying Rug? Lilypads? Starfish?

MA shakes her head. Takes two painkillers.

Can we do Track?

MA: There's no room to run in here.

GRAN: We could go outside – but no, sorry, the TV crews are still out there.

LITTLE JACK: Word sandwiches?

GRAN: You'd like a sandwich?

He shakes his head.

LITTLE JACK: *(To MA.)* Please, I want some.

MA: Not right now.

GRAN: What's that? What would you like, Jack? We've got everything.

MA: He wants to feed.

GRAN: You're not still…

MA: What?

GRAN: No, it's fine.

MA: You don't approve?

GRAN: I didn't say anything.

MA: You didn't have to. Why would I have stopped, in there?

GRAN: I know, sweetheart, I know.

MA: You don't know anything about it.

GRAN: *(Lowers her voice.)* Then tell me. Every detail, don't spare me.

MA: I don't want you to be thinking about that stuff every time you look at me.

GRAN: Every time I look at you I think hallelujah.

LITTLE JACK: *(To MA.)* Can we do Scream?

MA: There's nothing to scream about now!

He runs to her bedroom.

After a moment, MA goes after him.

GRANDAD ARRIVES

Later.

GRAN: *(Calling from below.)* He's here!

MA hurries downstairs. LITTLE JACK follows, on his bum.

MA: Dad!

GRANDAD: Oh my lovely. I can't believe it.

They embrace.

GRAN tries to lure LITTLE JACK away.

GRAN: Why don't we go have a snack?

He ignores her, eyes fixed on the stranger.

MA: *(To her dad.)* And here's Jack. Say hi to your Grandad.

LITTLE JACK mouths 'hi'. GRANDAD turns away, shakes his head.

BIG JACK: But I'm Jack. Was he expecting a different one?

GRANDAD: I told your mother, I'm not ready for... No offence.

MA: What do you mean, no offence?

GRAN: *(Pulling at LITTLE JACK's hand.)* Let's go see if we can find that hammock in the attic.

But he won't budge.

GRANDAD: I can't be in the same room. It makes me shudder.

MA: There's no 'it'. Jack's my little boy.

GRANDAD: I'm saying it wrong, I'm tired, OK?

MA: None of this is OK.

GRAN tries to fill the silence.

GRAN: You won't believe what a clever fellow Jack is – counts to a hundred, multiplies and everything, with a reading age of I don't know what.

GRANDAD: All I can think about is that bastard and what he did to my daughter.

MA: Would you rather I was in that coffin you buried?

GRANDAD: No!

MA: I've come home –

GRANDAD: It's a miracle.

MA: – with Jack, that's two miracles.

GRANDAD: My baby –

MA: He's *my* baby. He's the world to me. Look him in the eye.

BIG JACK: I think the he is me.

GRANDAD: *(To JACK, forcing himself.)* Pleased to meet you.

MA: Jack, manners.

LITTLE JACK: Thank you, you're welcome.

> *MA hauls LITTLE JACK away to her bedroom.*

> *GRAN goes over to GRANDAD. They lean on each other, broken.*

OUTSIDE

MA has earbuds in, listening to music. LITTLE JACK puts his head beside hers, trying to listen in. She pulls away. He yanks one bud out.

MA: Let me listen to my music.

> *She puts the buds back in and listens.*

LITTLE JACK: Why's it *your* music?

BIG JACK: Ma says everything's to share now, the house and the air and the streets. Why's the music not to share?

> *LITTLE JACK pulls the bud out again.*

> *MA turns the music off.*

MA: If I could just… Never mind. What do you want to do, then?

> *LITTLE JACK shrugs.*

Let's go outside. Where are your shoes?

LITTLE JACK: In the bin.

MA: Jack!

LITTLE JACK: They squish my feet.

MA: You're just not used to them yet, but you'll never get used to them unless you wear them.

She dresses them both.

LITTLE JACK: Sky's falling down in wet bits.

MA: That's just a sprinkle of rain, it won't hurt us. Look, there's a blue bit. I bet the Sun will come out soon.

BIG JACK: There's clouds with a big invisible wind chasing. We put on our sunglasses and sunhats so our faces don't burn off.

LITTLE JACK loses his nerve.

MA: Come on, Jack, don't you want to play in the garden? Why did we bother escaping if all we're going to do is sit cooped up inside?

LITTLE JACK: OK.

He goes down the stairs faster this time.

He and MA put on sunhats and sunglasses and start to go through the door...

LITTLE JACK panics and runs back indoors.

MA: What's wrong?

LITTLE JACK: Too much.

MA: Too much what?

LITTLE JACK: Too much everything.

MA: You're scared but you need to be brave, remember? Scave?

BIG JACK: I used up all my scave already, I'm just ordinary scared.

MA: One more try. Please? Pretend you're a boy in TV going for a walk with his Ma.

LITTLE JACK comes with her.

Outside, he breathes, begins to calm himself. He bends to touch the grass.

LITTLE JACK: Spiky.

MA: The grass? Yeah, it's never as soft as it looks. See that? It's an acorn. That'll grow and grow until it's a huge oak tree.

LITTLE JACK: Soon?

MA: *(Laughs.)* No, by the time you're a man.

LITTLE JACK: An alive thing.

MA: That's an ant.

LITTLE JACK: *(Shielding it.)* Don't smush it!

MA: I won't, I promise. Want to let it crawl over your finger?

She shows him how.

Do you hear all the alive things?

Bird song, a dog barking.

Then the whir of a helicopter. MA looks up and realises they're being filmed.

Run!

MA hustles him back indoors.

They tear off their sunglasses and sunhats.

EVIDENCE

POLICE is waiting for them at the table.

POLICE: Hello, Jack.

BIG JACK: It's the she from the night we escaped.

POLICE: *(To MA.)* We've made an arrest. I'd like to show you some photos, if you feel ready?

MA: After seven years, you think I'm going to crumble at a picture?

She looks at the pictures on the tablet.

LITTLE JACK: *(Peeking.)* Old Nick!

MA nods a confirmation, and turns it over.

POLICE: You're sure?

MA gives her a 'How-could-I-not-be-sure' look.

MA: *(To LITTLE JACK.)* They've locked him up.

LITTLE JACK: He can't come and get us?

MA: Never. Go on up to our room.

LITTLE JACK: With *you.*

MA: I'll be up in a minute.

LITTLE JACK goes, reluctantly.

POLICE: Let's go over your statement one more time.

MA rolls her eyes.

Any little thing you can remember, it's all evidence. Also we're going to need blood samples from both of you.

MA: More?

POLICE: For DNA this time.

MA: DNA? You don't believe Jack's his? You think there were other men?

POLICE: I think monsters get off on technicalities all the time.

SEVENTEEN DAYS AND A QUARTER

In the bedroom, LITTLE JACK is listening to music.

BIG JACK: We've been in the world for seventeen days and a quarter and I still never know what's going to hurt. Needles, and ice cream, and tables banging into me, and shoes, and doors trying to chop my fingers off. I met a bee, I tried to cuddle it and it stung me. Now the invisible germs have got up my nose and my brain's starting to melt and drip out. Ma's stressed all the time and I'm not to bother her, I have to give her space. I'm scared to go outside in case the helicopters get us. The Police locked Old Nick up but there are lots of other bad guys left in the world, so never never never go with a person not a friend, shout out 'Stranger danger, stranger danger!'

At night, I go in Room for dreaming. Just me, not Ma: it's a secret. I run around saying hello to all my friends. I flash Lamp and jump from Fridge to Bed to Wardrobe, I show them all how extra tall I've got in my seven-league shoes. But the friends are all forgetting how to talk. Plant's dried up from being so thirsty because we aren't in Room to give her water. Ma's not there in the dream, I don't know where she's hiding. Thermostat won't heat up the air. The water comes out freezing and it's spilling out of Bath, it's filling up all of Room and I'm drowning –

FAMILY FIGHT

A meal with the grandparents. LITTLE JACK's caught a cold.

GRAN: *(To MA.)* You're not eating your dad's curry.

MA: Yes I am.

GRANDAD: Not much of it.

MA: The way you all stuff yourselves, the sheer waste… No wonder the Earth's burning up.

GRANDAD: I think you'll see things differently when you've had a bit more sleep.

LITTLE JACK pushes his plate away.

LITTLE JACK: I want some.

MA: Not now.

LITTLE JACK: Please.

MA: I'm trying to eat here.

LITTLE JACK: I said please.

MA: You're not a baby anymore. And stop sniffing.

GRAN: *(To MA.)* Have a nap, maybe, before the TV people come?

GRANDAD: It's not too late to cancel this interview.

MA: *(To JACK.)* Blow your nose.

She holds out a tissue. He only wipes his nose.

GRAN: A quick nap, maybe?

MA: I've slept away seven years of my life. I'm not going to spend my time napping.

GRAN: Oh pet.

MA: I'm not your pet.

GRANDAD: You'll always be our little girl.

MA: Your little girl is dead and buried. You both got on with your lives, didn't you?

BIG JACK: Ma's not dead and buried!

LITTLE JACK sniffs again.

MA: Blow it like I showed you.

He tries, feebly.

Again!

LITTLE JACK: I can't.

MA: You're not trying.

> *He knocks the tissue away.*
>
> *GRAN picks it up.*

GRANDAD: *(To MA.)* You don't seem in any state to be going on television.

GRAN: Have you even told the doctor you're doing this interview?

GRANDAD: Is it for the money? Because that shouldn't matter, we can –

MA: *(Interrupts.)* Why don't you just fly back to your new home?

GRAN: Please, love. Call it off.

GRANDAD: Will I drive you somewhere? Want to go shopping? Ring up one of your old friends?

> *LITTLE JACK sniffs again.*

MA: Blow it!

GRAN: Go easy on the lad.

> *She wipes his nose.*

(To LITTLE JACK.) You're like a visitor from another planet, that's why you've caught a cold.

BIG JACK: We're not visitors. Ma says we have to live here forever and ever till we're dead.

MA: I need to get ready.

> *She rushes to her room. LITTLE JACK follows.*

Give me a minute.

LITTLE JACK: No going in TV without me.

MA: I'm doing this for us, Jack. We need money so we can get out of this house.

LITTLE JACK: Let me go in TV with you.

MA: Would you just give me ten minutes to get my head together?

LITTLE JACK: Ten minutes *with* me.

MA: Get the hell out of my room!

She shoves him away.

I JUST WANNA BE FOUR AGAIN SONG

BIG JACK: People say 'welcome home'.
Stupid adults get it wrong again.
Home is Room and
Room's where I belong.

People say 'Do you like being free?'
Stupid people, they don't see,
How's it free when
Everything is rules?

In outside everything belongs
To somebody else.
You have to pay or police come quick
To put you in the jail.

There's all these rules
That I don't know
But if I break them they get mad.
I don't understand,
I did what Ma asked,
So how's it I am bad?

I don't like being big,
I don't like being free.
I wish I could go back
To just Ma and me.

To Room where it's safe,
To Room where I'm free,
I don't wanna grow up,
I just wanna be four again.

I wish I'd said no, no,
Said no way Jose!
I wish that today
Could just be yesterday.
I'll get me a rocket,
I'll fly it so fast.
I'll travel through time and
I'll get to the past.

I don't wanna grow up,
I just wanna be four again.
I don't wanna grow up,
I just wanna be four again.
I don't wanna grow up,
I just wanna be four again.

INTERVIEW

BIG JACK: Gran's house is full of everybody talking and moving about and lights and machines.

CAMERAPERSON: Live in two minutes.

BIG JACK: There's a woman with shiny hair with a box of colours, she's painting her face.

INTERVIEWER: The boy's not to be shown on camera. No snapshots for personal use.

BIG JACK: And a person counting 5, 4, 3, 2, 1, is there going to be a rocket?

INTERVIEWER: *(On video.)* She was only nineteen, the girl next door, when a brutal stranger dubbed the Gardenshed

Ogre kidnapped, drugged, raped and imprisoned her. In this exclusive interview in her childhood home, the young mother of the Bonsai Boy breaks her silence, speaking out for the first time about those seven lost years.

LITTLE JACK eavesdrops on the interview.

INTERVIEWER: On that cold day, you gave birth alone under medieval conditions. Was that the hardest thing you've ever done?

MA: The best thing.

INTERVIEWER: Well, that too, of course.

MA: I was alive again, I mattered. So after that I was polite, like some Stepford Wife.

INTERVIEWER: You mean with your captor?

MA: *(Nods.)* I had to keep Jack safe.

INTERVIEWER: Now raising him all on your own, without family or books or professionals, that must have been terribly difficult.

MA: I think a baby just wants to have his mother right there.

INTERVIEWER: *(Nods.)* You breastfed him. In fact, this may shock some of our viewers, but I understand you still do?

MA: In this whole story, *that's* the shocking detail?

INTERVIEWER: Oh but nobody's judging you. The emails and tweets that have been pouring in – you do realise you're a beacon of hope to women everywhere?

MA: I'm no saint. All I did was survive. I wish people would stop treating us like we're the only ones who ever lived through something terrible. People are locked up in all sorts of ways.

INTERVIEWER: Now, you came to what some experts are calling a strange decision, to teach him that there was nothing outside that hellhole of a shed. Did you ever feel bad that you were deceiving Jack?

MA: What was I meant to tell him – hey, there's a whole world out there and you can't touch it?

INTERVIEWER: You must have been tortured by all the pleasures you couldn't give him.

MA: Well – yeah – but – he seemed happy.

INTERVIEWER: Now you've been rescued –

MA: *(Interrupts.)* Escaped. We rescued ourselves.

INTERVIEWER: Indeed you did. Do you ever find that looking at Jack painfully reminds you of his biological father?

MA: No!

INTERVIEWER: These days, do you sometimes miss the simplicities and certainties of living behind a locked door?

MA: That's ridiculous.

INTERVIEWER: Would you say you feel an almost pathological need to stand guard between Jack and the world?

MA: It's called being a mother.

INTERVIEWER: Given his many 'differences', do you believe he'll ever entirely adjust to society and become a normal little boy?

MA: I – I don't – I think I've had enough.

INTERVIEWER: Just one final question, if I may. When Jack was born, some have wondered why you never considered asking your captor to take him away, to leave him outside a hospital perhaps. It would have been the ultimate sacrifice, of course, but if he could have been adopted – as you were yourself – if he could have had a healthy childhood with a loving family – if all these years, he could have been free…

MA'S LULLABY

Alone in her room, MA takes an overdose.

MA: Being confused and being afraid,
    You were not brought up that way.
    Fold me up and put me away.
    Save yourself for safer days.

    I built you out of milk and lies,
    Fed you all I had inside.
    I have poisoned your little mind.
    To take me out is to be kind.

BIG JACK: Me and Ma are in the sea,
    So deep down,
    Tangled in her hair,
    I can't breathe.
    I try to scream.
    'Wake up Ma!'
    Wake up Ma!
    She can't hear me.

MA: Loving you has made me live
    Inside Room but out of it.
    This new life for you is too strange.
    Save yourself for safer ways.

    You are everything that's right,
    Beautiful and made of light.
    You will shine more bright if I'm gone,
    Save yourself for safer songs.

    I'm all dried up,
    I'm all washed up.
    I cannot feed you,
    I cannot feed you.

    I did my best.

My best's not enough.
The mess I will make.
Don't let me wake.

I did my best.
Still I fucked up.
I'm all dried up.
I'm all washed up.

Don't let me wake,
Don't let me wake,
Don't let me wake,
Don't let me wake…

BIG JACK: Me and Ma are in the sea,
So deep down,
Tangled in her hair,
I can't breathe.
I try to scream.
'Wake up Ma!'
Wake up Ma!
She can't hear me.
Wake up Ma!

LITTLE JACK: Ma!

WITHOUT MA

LITTLE JACK is curled up in misery.

GRAN: Listen to me.

LITTLE JACK: Where is she really?

GRAN: I told you, they took her to Casualty.

LITTLE JACK: Why are you pretending she's alive?

GRAN: I'm not, I swear.

LITTLE JACK: If Ma's not alive, I don't want to be.

GRAN: But she is, or she was when they took her in the ambulance. They'll fix her.

Phone rings. GRAN hurries off.

GRANDAD comes in.

GRANDAD: You all right, Jack? She did a stupid thing, taking all those tablets. She wouldn't have done it if she'd been herself.

LITTLE JACK: Who is she then?

GRANDAD: I don't know, it's all too much for me. I hardly know her anymore.

GRAN comes back, in tears.

GRAN: I'll get him. He's right here. Jack? Phone for you. It's her, it's your Ma!

LITTLE JACK holds the receiver near his ear but far from his mouth.

LITTLE JACK: Hello?

GRANDAD moves it nearer JACK's mouth and gestures for him to repeat it.

Hello?

MA'S VOICE: Jack! Jack, I'm sorry. I'm so sorry.

LITTLE JACK hunches around the phone, wanting to be private.

LITTLE JACK: Why didn't you wait?

MA'S VOICE: What?

LITTLE JACK: Why didn't you wait for me and take me to Heaven too?

MA'S VOICE: I'm not in Heaven, I'm at the hospital.

LITTLE JACK: Come back.

MA'S VOICE: I wish I –

LITTLE JACK: *(Interrupts.)* I wish double. You come back and everything be hunky-dory.

MA'S VOICE: The doctors are trying to figure out what I need, the dosage.

LITTLE JACK: Me. You need *me.*

MA'S VOICE: Soon, I'll be there as soon as I can.

LITTLE JACK: Not soon, now!

MA'S VOICE: Jack!

LITTLE JACK: *I* choose. I choose for both of us.

MA'S VOICE: I can't –

LITTLE JACK drops the phone and stumbles away.

SHOPPING CENTRE

BIG JACK: Mind over matter, mind over matter, but it does matter and I do mind. So I suck on Bad Tooth all the days till I'm all bad too. I watch TV that Gran calls the goggle box, I watch till my brain's all rotted. Little freak. All the days are Gone Days. I don't have any jobs to do, I don't have any friends, I don't have any superpowers, I don't have Ma because she tried to sneak into Heaven without me and the aliens threw her down and broke her to bits.

LITTLE JACK follows his GRANDPARENTS, at a distance. He sucks on MA's Bad Tooth.

GRAN: Oh look, there's a little playground.

GRANDAD: I thought you said you had to get to work?

GRAN: They'll understand if I'm a bit late. The boy needs to learn to play. Come on, Jack.

LITTLE JACK shakes his head.

Fresh air and other kids. Look, they're climbing the climbers and swinging on the swings and sliding down the slides, don't you fancy trying that?

GRANDAD: Let's buy the boy this bike then.

GRAN: All right. *(To LITTLE JACK.)* This is called a shopping centre. Hold hands?

He won't. They go in.

BIG JACK: The shopping centre's extra bright and ginormous, I didn't know inside could be as big as outside. There's trees even. But when I go up close and stroke them they're plastic. Lots of the world is pretend. There's a fountain that persons throw money in, it's a rubbish. Gran gives me a money to throw away.

GRAN: Make a wish. Wish for whatever you'd like best in the world.

BIG JACK: What I wish is Room with Ma and being four again, but that's not in the world.

GRAN: Now throw it.

LITTLE JACK throws the coin.

Want a snack, Jack?

He shakes his head.

GRANDAD: Ten minutes, you said.

GRAN: But what if he's hungry, or thirsty? Jack? Or what about a new book?

BIG JACK / LITTLE JACK: Alice!

LITTLE JACK runs towards a copy of 'Alice in Wonderland'. Then recoils as he sees there are many copies.

BIG JACK: Lots of Alice. Millions and millions.

GRAN: Would you like that book, sweetheart?

GRANDAD: Unless it's a bit old for him.

GRAN: *(To LITTLE JACK.)* What's that you're sucking on, a bead?

BIG JACK: Bad Tooth. That's a bit of Ma.

GRAN: Whatever it is, give it to Gran.

GRANDAD: Leave him be.

GRAN: It could choke the boy. Jack, give it here –

> *He wriggles away. She tries to take it out of his mouth and he resists, biting her.*

GRAN: Ow! You little monster.

GRANDAD: Hey, hey –

BIG JACK: You're the monster, ugly zombie monster!

BIG JACK / LITTLE JACK: Stranger danger, stranger danger!

> *LITTLE JACK has a howling, convulsive tantrum.*

GRAN: *(To GRANDAD.)* Are you just going to stand there?

GRANDAD: What do you want me to do?

GRAN: He's your bloody grandson!

> *GRANDAD picks LITTLE JACK up gently but firmly in a firefighter's lift.*

What are you doing?

> *LITTLE JACK screams and thumps GRANDAD's back.*

Put him down!

GRANDAD: He's all right.

> *LITTLE JACK's frenzy lulls. Sobbing now. GRANDAD rubs his back.*

Going to be all right.

LITTLE JACK rests his face on GRANDAD's shoulder.

LEGOS

At home, GRANDAD sets him down and gets out some Legos. He starts building a little house. He hands it to LITTLE JACK.

GRANDAD: C'mon, you make something now.

LITTLE JACK picks up a single plank-like piece.

LITTLE JACK: What if I break it?

GRANDAD: Can't be done. Press another one onto the little bumps.

LITTLE JACK: Do you still want me not born?

GRANDAD: What's that?

LITTLE JACK: You were angry Ma had a baby, that was me. Would you rather there's no me?

GRANDAD: I would not! Now stick a wheel on the end of that.

LITTLE JACK does.

Another one, other end.

LITTLE JACK does.

Skateboard!

LITTLE JACK bursts out laughing.

GRANDAD crunches the house and the skateboard in his fists.

LITTLE JACK is horrified.

Now we start again.

They do.

MA COMES HOME

MA comes in with a cast on her wrist and watches them.

LITTLE JACK sees her and runs over for a long hug.

LITTLE JACK: Are you better, Ma?

MA: I'm...much better. All the better for being home with you.

LITTLE JACK: But your wrist.

MA: The doctor broke it again so it would heal straight this time, isn't that funny?

LITTLE JACK: Is it all better now?

MA: Better than when it was bad. Everybody's a bit broken.

LITTLE JACK: Like Legos! Look, you crunch it and it's OK, you just make something else.

BIG JACK: Oh and I went on a swing and a boy was swinging right beside me at the same time. There was a poo of a dog but I didn't stand in it. And I have a bike! But I can't find Bad Tooth. I think maybe I swallowed him by accident when I was asleep. Hey, and I go down stairs standing up now. There's a trick, I just let myself start falling a bit, and stick my foot out and I'm up again.

LITTLE JACK: Gran's going to teach me to swim and not drown.

MA: Wow.

LITTLE JACK: Can I have some?

He goes to lift up her top.

MA: Jack. There's no more left.

LITTLE JACK: All gone?

MA: All gone.

LITTLE JACK: *(Touches her chest.)* Bye some.

MA: Maybe when you were small, there's things I should have
– some of what I did, before we got out, and after, I didn't
see any other way… I haven't been a good enough Ma.

LITTLE JACK: *(Doesn't understand her worry.)* But you're Ma.

She holds him tight.

MA: I've been thinking: we should try everything in the world
once so we'll know what we like.

LITTLE JACK: OK. Let's go in an airplane to see Grandad's
other house.

MA: *(Points at herself.)* Go back to uni. *(Points at him.)* Go to
school.

LITTLE JACK: Put up the hammock when it's summer.

BIG JACK: Me and Ma write a list. Ma's going to learn to drive
a car. I'll have a birthday cake with six candles really on
fire. And lots of friends. And our real dog called Lucky.
We'll live in a place of our own. Our place will have one
door that says 'Jack's Room' and one door that says 'Ma's
Room' but the doors will be open. We'll go to Sun and
Moon and all the Planets and all over the Earth.

LITTLE JACK: And go back to Room.

MA is shaken by that.

Just to visit.

BIG JACK: Plant's thirsty. And Labyrinth and Sockdog and
Eggsnake and Wonky Chair and Meltedy Spoon, they must be
lonely. Nobody's singing them songs or telling them stories.

MA: Jack…

LITTLE JACK: Just one time.

MA makes herself nod.

RETURN TO ROOM

Sound of rain.

LITTLE JACK: Rain's going to wet us.

MA: So we'll be wet. Come on, Jack, you asked to go back to Room.

LITTLE JACK: Maybe when I'm six.

MA: It has to be today.

LITTLE JACK: Maybe another day when there's no rain.

MA: Today. Because tomorrow they're going to knock it down.

LITTLE JACK: Knock down Room?

MA: See that bulldozer? After tomorrow there won't be a Room anymore.

THE GOODBYE ROOM SONG

BIG JACK: A ribbon squared marks the spot,
    Crime scene tape, a garden plot,
    Big, bold letters, DO NOT CROSS,
    That's everyone except us.

    We cross the line, go back in time.
    Ma bites her nails and shuts her eyes.
    She holds me close and water trickles
    Down her face to mine.

MA: The scars he gave me I own.
    The scars he gave me I own.

    Tall thick bushes all around,
    A shallow hole marks this ground,
    A hasty, dirty grave where they
    Found her baby bones.

75

The scars he gave me I own.
The scars he gave me I own.

BIG JACK /MA: Then we see the metal door,
    Electronic lock,
    The still stained floor,
    A thin, dark dust on everything.
    We silently go in.

BIG JACK: Say goodbye Floor,
    Goodbye Plant,
    Goodbye Wardrobe,
    Goodbye Eggsnake,
    Goodbye Lamp,
    Goodbye Sockdog,
    Goodbye Chair,
    Goodbye Labyrinth,
    Goodbye Skylight,
    Goodbye Room...

MA: The scars he gave me I own.
    The scars he gave me I own.

BIG JACK / MA: We take one last look,
    Me and Ma/Jack,
    We take one last look,
    Me and Ma/Jack,
    Then walk right out the door.
    We walk right out the door.
    We walk right out the door.

Lightning Source UK Ltd.
Milton Keynes UK
UKHW020642061021
391751UK00006B/140